Tangible Remains

Tangible Remains

Selected Poems

Linda Principe

Full Court Press
Englewood Cliffs, New Jersey

First Edition

Copyright © 2011 by Linda Principe

All rights reserved. No part of this book may be reproduced or transmitted in any form or by any means electronic or mechanical, including by photocopying, by recording, or by any information storage and retrieval system, without the express permission of the author and publisher, except where permitted by law.

Published in the United States of America
by Full Court Press, 601 Palisade Avenue
Englewood Cliffs, NJ 07632
www.fullcourtpressnj.com

ISBN 978-0-9837411-5-2
Library of Congress Control No. 2011943378

Editing and Book Design by Barry Sheinkopf for Bookshapers
(www.bookshapers.com)
Cover Photograph by Debbie Mazzei
Colophon by Liz Sedlack

Appearances of "Interlude of Rain" in the Summer 2003 issue, "Where Quarrels End" in the Fall 2003 issue, and "Eternity" in the Winter 2004 issue of *Vermont Ink,* are gratefully acknowledged.

FOR THE KID ON THE CORNER
who always believed
in the spaces
between stars.

For the poet
the poem
is not
the measure
of his love. It is
the measure
of all he's lost, or
never seen,
or what has no life
until he gives it life
with words.
—*Diane Wakoski*

Foreword

"An ant is an insect that crawls on the ground.
He hurries and scurries without making a sound."

These were the first lines of poetry I ever wrote. I was seven years old and in the first grade. The poem was published in the school's literary journal. Oh, the excitement of seeing those words in print was like waking up on Christmas morning to discover Santa had left you everything you requested. I still have that book and look at it whenever I want to remember what unadulterated joy feels like.

At thirteen, I picked up a pen and that is when my real love affair with words began in earnest. I loved the fire in my soul, when I looked at something, and words would suddenly ignite in my mind. I would write for hours, during the night, when all good thirteen-year-olds should be sleeping, the variety of colored inks from my plastic Schaeffer fountain pens forming a rainbow across my fingers.

Throughout my life, poetry has been a way to capture my evolving selves. When the world fell apart, words made it whole. When nothing made sense, words created meaning and a context. When I was a stranger to myself, words led me home. As I dealt with chronic illness, deaths, and murders, words kept me anchored and sane. Writing has saved my life more times than I can count, and words have accompanied me on my most joyous of journeys and into the deepest corners of despair. Every self I have ever been, for better or worse, is on the pages of countless notebooks. What I see when I read back is the evolution of who I was, who I am, and a slow progression toward everything I was ever meant to be.

As I prepared the poems for this collection, I tried to choose those that reflect, most honestly, the roads I've walked, a view that encompasses the New Brighton streets that shaped me, as well as, the moments of love, laughter and loss that, strung together, represent life as I've known it. The most magical thing about a poem is that it can give you back a moment lost and allow you to understand yourself and your place in, what seems, at best, an indifferent universe. Poetry is not just a craft; it's a way of seeing the world. That "kid on the corner" gazing up at the stars knew that, even then. She understood the transformative power of words, and *Tangible Remains* is a gift from this me to that me, the fulfillment of a destiny she grasped long before I did.

When I saw my first words in print at age seven, I felt a sense of accomplishment and excitement, but I didn't have the words to express how it really felt to hold that book in my hands. At fifty, as I hold this book in my hands, I still don't.

—L.P.
Staten Island, October 2011

Table of Contents

The Summoning, *1*
The Poetry of Echoes, *3*
Back to the Streets, *4*
The Fluttering, *6*
Sacrificing Street Corners, *7*
Sole Asylum, *9*
Big Shoes to Fill, *11*
Wood You Believe, *13*
The Wilderness Within, *15*
Return to Summer, *16*
Thirty Steps to Heaven, *18*
My Grandmother's Mint, *20*
Grandpa's Wine, *22*
Picking Peaches, *24*
On the Tip of My Tongue, *26*
New Brighton Snowfall, *28*
Enter at Your Own Risk, *30*
Slats, *32*
Walking in a Storm, *33*
Dancing up a Storm, *35*
Broken by Love, *37*
Headstones, *39*
Accidental Picasso, *41*
Impending October, *43*
Color Coordinated, *44*
Of All Things, *46*
Gulls, *47*
Cliff Hanger, *48*
Driven by Joy, *50*

Where the Stars Go, *52*
Rooftops, *53*
The Snowball, *55*
Sand and Snow, *57*
Ferris Wheel, *58*
Dead Man's Hill, *59*
Downhill from Here, *61*
Black Fence, *63*
The Door Bell, *65*
The Dance, *66*
Affirmation, *67*
Editing Love, *68*
Dress Rehearsal, *69*
Never Mind the Moon, *70*
The Music of My Heart, *71*
Music Lesson, *72*
The Unraveling of Days, *73*
The Things You Taught Me, *75*
Empty Closets, *77*
All the Words in the World, *79*
When Seasons Change, *80*
September Falling, *82*
Spring Thaw, *84*
Today's Lesson, *86*
A Million Dreams, *88*
More Tree than Flower, *90*
Synchronized Swimming, *91*
To Say the Least, *93*
Heart Beat in the Hollow, *95*
Holding the Light, *97*
Tumbling through Centuries, *99*
Never Far, *101*

Testament, *103*
The Dark Shape of Trees, *104*
A Gift to the Stars, *106*
No Ghost, *108*
The Promise of Bridges, *110*
Latitude, *112*
Magnificent Desolation, *114*
Graffiti on the Sky, *116*
What a Poem Feels Like, *117*
The First Sound, *118*
Stranger to Stranger, *120*
Where Mountains Weep, *122*
Undiluted Starlight, *124*
The Symphony of Trees, *126*
About Tulips, *128*
Eclipse of Reason, *129*
Pieces of You, *131*
Geography of My Existence, *133*
Eternity, *135*
Interlude of Rain, *136*
Where Quarrels End, *137*
Choreography, *138*
Pennies from Heaven, *139*
Paper, *140*
Tangible Remains, *142*

The Summoning

Chosen
as scribe to the whispering voice
that entered my soul uninvited,

that first line crosses my mind like a banner
flapping off the back of a plane
in a summer blue sky:
"When they were mad and left me alone..."
It came,
an unexpected breeze that became my breath.

Beckoned
by something more stranger than muse,
the spell was cast, and I was captive
to vision and voice, addicted to ink,
captured by the unwritten poem
on every blank page I saw.

Stolen
from amid the crowd
as steamy day slipped into silky night,
I, too, slipped into a place where stars danced
and the heavens sang
songs only I could hear.

Chosen
as the instrument of a muse whose name I never knew,
a poet was born,
my nights given over to words,

the only surrender in my life
that didn't diminish me.

Summoned
I have been singing ever since.

THE POETRY OF ECHOES

Why go back to moments,
over and done,
to sunlit days and electric nights?

Why return
to what you'll never be again,
to mourn time's thievery
and what passes before you like reels of film
clicking towards darkness?

Why not write now,
        right now
of life happening,
the freshly blossoming flower
instead of dry petals pressed
between pages of books?

Books go out of print; memories don't.
That is the magnetic pull of the past,
when the present really was poetry,
and the future, sounds I hadn't made yet.
In the end,
it is all the poetry of echoes,
moments reverberating in the soul,
memories bouncing off walls
like rays of sun in a vacant room.

The past is magic
not because it cannot be rewritten —
simply because it doesn't need to be.

Back to the Streets

If things hadn't changed,
I'd return to the streets that shaped me
just to see, again,
the welcoming light in my grandmother's windows.

I'd sit on the brick steps,
watch the shadows of children,
now grown with kids of their own,
play on the grass, the grime of the day
in the creases of their hands
as they stomp inside for their baths.

I'd walk the path into the woods,
hear the echo of dueling boom boxes,
one thumping disco,
the other screaming rock,
and taste the beer that would drown out all sound
still on my tongue.

I'd go to the church
they carried my grandma's blue casket from,
feel my eyes tear from the sun gleaming on metal
(or so I told myself),
and remember one of the most desolate moments
I have ever known.

On my corner in total silence, I'd stare into the sky;
and if someone came along and asked me
if I'd lost something, I'd say,

Yes, myself,
but I know I'm here somewhere—
> everywhere, in fact.

The Fluttering

I wrote by open windows,
pages rustling in the soft breeze,
a street light the only light
separating me
from the oblivion of night.

Armed with words,
I warred on the foreign soil
of love and loss,
battled enemies real and imagined,
my pen the only refuge I had
from an indifferent world.

Hour by hour, I scribbled,
sometimes until that orange sliver of day
rose above the house on the corner
where my deepest dreams
simply waited politely by the door
for an invitation that would never come.

In the stillness of this night,
I hear it like my own breath
in the silence,
the fluttering of my heart,
the fluttering of those pages
on summer winds at midnight
in a place where wishes were a dime a dozen,
and I had plenty of dimes.

SACRIFICING STREET CORNERS

Sentinel of the night,
guardian of youthful dreams—
to most, nothing more
than a telephone pole
on a now-empty street corner.

Poems found their way to pages
beneath the curve of that light,
amid friends and first loves,
the buzzing of the lamp, a sound
I can still hear on silent summer nights.

My spine in many storms,
I leaned against that solid wood
on the cold October morning that changed my life,
alone with my adolescent thoughts
and tears that would not come.

Strong and weathered,
part of the place I called home,
here where hours unwound into years
and years into absences,
irretrievable pieces of what we lose
on the road to maturity.

Through time, the wood splintered
and the pole tilted to the left,
but still it stood,
like me.

The words born beneath that hazy light
were dreams I could afford to believe in
before I understood the passing of youth
and the sacrificing of street corners
for more practical pursuits.

SOLE ASYLUM

Kelly green like the leaves
of adolescent springtimes,
that was the color
of my magic sneakers.

They accompanied me
on all the roads I walked,
up every tree I climbed,
through all the puddles I pounced in.
I wrote my first lines of poetry
on the white soles,
so struck by the fire of a moment
I couldn't wait for paper.

I chose green
so I'd blend with my surroundings.
Perhaps I'd be mistaken for the grass I stood on,
and flowers would bloom from my head—
as bloom they did, in notebooks I filled
fast and furious, in the heat of a midday sun,
by a streetlight amid blaring music,
by the light of a midnight moon
shining through the porch windows.
Sensitive to passing time,
I wrote knowing every moment was final,
the dying of youth,
the birth of an adult
with different dreams and more acceptable shoes.
I wore those kelly green Pro-Keds

on my frequent trips to the stars.

Maybe they declared
my sense of difference—
selfhood on my feet
instead of my heart on my sleeve.

Big Shoes to Fill

I lived in those sneakers—
green, red, black, blue, white,
all with those two stripes on the sole
that defined them
and me.

Dictates of season meant nothing.
I wore them in snow,
impervious to my frozen toes.
Once they went numb,
the pain ceased anyway.

Time demands change,
and I can't say exactly when,
but somewhere along the way,
I surrendered those sneakers
and then they disappeared

until last year when they appeared online.
I had to have them so placed the order,
same size I was all those years ago.
When they arrived,
it was like part of the past
returned to sender,
memories delivered courtesy of UPS.

I put them on and smiled
until, suddenly,
they began to hurt

in the back, on the sides.
After several futile attempts
to break them in,
I gave up and put them in the closet.

Had they changed or had I?
Strange that I can't even fill my own shoes;
but then, maybe there are simply roads
I wasn't meant to walk again.

Wood You Believe

Wood chippings at twilight,
on the edge of sunset,
that moment before the moment
becomes another day.
Fiery streaks on the lake,
the sun dipped, drowning its sorrows
in still water.
I was full of fire then, too—
burning with youth,
desire I had no name for,
the need to fly above the life I knew
into dreams I believed I could fulfill
by sheer will and poetry.

That sense of freedom prompted me
to take out my pocket knife,
fearlessness only children possess
guiding my hand as I carved names and a date
into an aging blue bench
bottom, left-hand corner.
My fingers ached from the effort,
but I worked until it was done,
the only way to create in wood,
a union that life would never allow me.

Today, I carve with pen into paper.
The fingers still ache,
but I will not rest until I've proven
that forever is more than some fairy tale.

Wood splinters, the names now long gone,
but the feeling's alive, well, and inscribed on pages
neither weather nor world can touch.

Strange to rise above the life I knew,
simply to find it was the only one
I ever really wanted.

THE WILDERNESS WITHIN

When I close my eyes,
I see a young child running
like a stallion through the days,
dirt caked in the creases of my hands,
the taste of my own sweat as I fielded a ball
no one was supposed to catch.

I knew, even then, I was meant for other things.

When I bled at thirteen, I clenched my thighs
to stem the flow of impending womanhood
as if I could prevent some part of me
from ebbing out.
How the terror filled me as I reflected on
what would happen -
I'd be gripped by a sudden desire to wear dresses,
no longer one of the boys, but one of the boys'.
My fingernails would sprout, and my baseball glove
would never fit right again—
the imaginings of a child afraid of losing
the wilderness within.

As I watch you polish your nails,
I smile, for here I am, at forty-nine,
comfortable in my well-worn jeans,
staring at my stubby-nailed fingers,
contemplating what I knew deep inside then,
what I know even better now:
My baseball glove is still a perfect fit.

Return to Summer

The wind shifts;
the deepening orange of the sky
as twilight descends informs me
that another season's on its way.

I carry a thousand summers inside,
memories wound around my heart like ribbon
on unopened gifts.

Starlit skies from golden days
glitter in my mind, brighter despite passing time;
yesterday's breezes,
the breath that filled my lungs,
ruffled my pages until I responded
and set loose the words like balloons;
laughter in the night air,
voices of children running wild,
the thud of a ball volleying
across the street and back,
melted to silence
after everyone had gone and we sat
gazing at the heavens as if what we sought
was out there.

What were we looking for,
and did we ever find it?

Or could it be that what we needed
was right there all along,

in you, in me,
in the history created on nights like that
when the return to summer
was more about making memories
than about remembering?

Thirty Steps to Heaven

When I was six,
my grandfather rescued a pigeon
fallen from the roof.
This injured creature blinked
in beady-eyed questioning
as Grandpa wrapped its wing,
white cloth, a makeshift sling,
cardboard box, a temporary home.

Tucked in a warm corner of the cellar,
every day I'd run there to converse.
I'd never seen a pigeon up that close.
Dirty birds, my mother'd say
when I chased them across sidewalks.
But this didn't look like a dirty bird to me.

Grateful for the company, her gray feathers
quivered beneath my small hand,
and in that moment my desire for flight was born.
She'd seen a world I'd only dreamed of,
reached places I hadn't even imagined yet,
the idea incarnate, long before I had words
to express it.

Then one day, an empty box;
I searched that cellar, end to end,
cried, and accused Grandpa of eating my friend.

Two days later, we found her in the attic,

spindly legs in the air, stiff as a board.
They said she'd died of a broken wing,
but, in my six-year-old way, I knew
she'd died of desire—
she needed to fly,
had walked up thirty steps to glimpse the sky
just once more
before she accepted
her limitations.

My Grandmother's Mint

The smell of mint on the summer air,
the magic carpet that sails me
into the memory of my grandmother's yard:

In front of the crooked, boulder-bespeckled wall,
stood neat rows of plants,
green-tuxedoed dandies whose cologne
saturated every inch of wind.

On any given day, I could follow my nose
from three houses up and find my way home
with my eyes closed.

Through windows and doors,
through all the pores of the house,
that fragrance permeated:

the carefully hidden pack of cigarettes,
menthol, of course,
I got caught plucking from there;
all the other carefully guarded treasures
that didn't give themselves up as easily
as smoke rings.

My grandmother's mint,
like all her other flowers,
was meant to endure.
And it does.
And it will

as long as there are summer winds to carry it,
to carry me home.
I follow my nose, with my eyes closed,
from three houses up
and thirty years away,
I still get there.
Every time.

Grandpa's Wine

Stacked one upon the other,
wooden crates were tucked
in the shady alcove beneath the stairs,
stamped on the side
Imported from Italy.
Cached inside were the grapes
from a foreign land that would be pressed and bottled
into Grandpa's wine.

Against all warnings,
I'd sneak to the yard, open a box, and pull out
a handful of heaven;
in the furthest corner, I'd sit beneath
the blazing sky of my childhood
and eat those grapes,
one at a time.

Perfectly round,
amazingly sweet and unwashed,
they were better than candy.
Before long, the stains of my thievery
appeared like bruises on my lips,
on my small fingers.
I learned how to be purple long before
I learned how to be blue.

Remembering that sweetness,
the innocence of stolen grapes
from the foreign land called the past,

my heart aches to taste, again,
a time when the grapes were better than good enough,
and I never needed the wine
to get drunk.

Picking Peaches

Thump, thump,
thud, thud—
sounds of mid-summer that echo
in my heart;
Peach-picking time,
from the huge tree in the side yard
of my grandmother's house.

I watched that fruit multiply daily
from the windows of the second floor,
amazed that, suddenly one day,
there were more than I could count.

Then came the magic words,
Go pick-a-the-peaches,
and out I'd go out with my dad,
he with the ladder,
I with the bushels.
He'd climb to the top,
start shaking the limbs,
and my life on the ground suddenly
became a game of dodge ball,
hard, round objects flying all around me.
I was always bruised afterward;
the fruit never was.

The lumps on my head ached,
but far worse was the itch—
the fuzz of those peaches, like shards of fiberglass,

would set your skin on fire upon contact,
a burning even water couldn't wash away,

Several hours later,
bushel upon bushel of peaches lay at my feet;
tired, sweaty, and sore,
I'd glance up at grandma's face in the window,
smiling, and it was all worth it—
the good harvest of childhood,
the great harvest of memory
that still makes me itch.

On the Tip of My Tongue

Walking into the local store,
sawdust on wooden floors,
you must have strolled down the aisles,
with one child or another on your arm,
searching the shelves and bins
for what you needed.

You knew what you wanted,
what it looked like, the purpose it served,
but you simply didn't have the word for it;
you thought in Italian,
spoke in broken English,
and the laughter often born
of the discrepancy rises in me,
even now.

This day occurred long before I was born,
but I'd have given anything
to experience that priceless moment
when you asked the salesperson
for the *thing*,
you know, *the thing where*
water go,
macaroni stop.

A lifetime down the line,
your daughters passed that story on,
and the feeling it gave me,
the feeling it gave me—

well, it's on the tip of my tongue:
Grandma go,
memory never stop.

New Brighton Snowfall

The shadow of me
I see vividly—
the lone figure I was walking slowly,
a New Brighton street in the silence
of falling snow.

Back then, venturing alone was safe
as I searched every corner of night for peace
and my breath rose and dissipated,
unlike that unending, insensible feeling
inside me.

I recall that quiet,
how I wished it would sink into me
and muffle the clash of words in my head
as I struggled to suppress them
and their realizations.

I looked at the sky,
flakes landing softly on my eyelashes, and knew
I couldn't hold back any more than the sky could.

I stopped on a corner
and stood still in the snow,
the only soul in the universe,
wondering if love would always mean suffering,
if suffering was the only path to the words
I wrote that didn't melt.

No one will ever know
how much of me is still there
on that street waiting for it to stop—
snowing.

Enter at Your Own Risk

Down the block and across the street,
Malandro's, the neighborhood store,
sat nestled amid a continuous row of houses,
green wooden door with nine square panes of glass
that should have had a sign :
Enter at Your Own Risk.

Back then, a dollar could buy a pack of butts,
no proof required,
and leave enough change
for a Coke and Yankee Doodles.

I could hear Jimmy and Chick
screaming long before I reached the store,
wondering what they always found to fight about.

Sawdust swirled on the floor as I opened the door
and headed straight for the cubby holes of candy—
BB Bats, Buttons, and Bazooka,
all a penny apiece
when half a buck bought a lot of cavities.
I'd step out, reach into my brown bag,
and start chomping as I walked.
Whoever believes I cannot walk and chew gum
at the same time didn't know me then.

Often, I'd look behind
and see tomatoes or potatoes rocketing
across the store as those two brothers

waged war, voices wafting in the hot air,
lingering like a distant song.

It was all so simple and clear
when penny candy actually cost a penny,
when it was safe to walk home alone
and your friends were your friends
even on days when you didn't like each other.
There was no problem
a piece of gum couldn't remedy.

Slats

I always called it the Little House,
though the origin of the name escapes me.
A square on a slab of concrete,
constructed of wood, walls of 2-inch slats,
painted and splintering green,
it sat beside my grandma's house,
this place where I memorized the dances
of shadows on cement.

The perimeter was all bench,
my favorite spot in the far corner
where I'd sit and watch the world move,
the young poet in training,
learning to observe
away, apart, and alone.

I don't know its history
except that my grandfather built it,
and if I close my eyes,
I can still feel the intermittent rays of sun through slats
on my face as I lay on the bench glancing
at strips of sky.

Dreaming is not my heritage,
no cloud walkers in my lineage,
but I learned to dream in that Little House,
and the day I climbed on the roof,
right before they knocked it down,
I saw the world clearer than I ever have since.

Walking in a Storm

The curbs were rivers,
streams of water so strong
I had to lean forward to move—
so powerful, it breached the curbs
and sheeted down the sidewalk
like some angry god had turned on a faucet
and simply walked away.

Rain pelted my face,
stinging like peas shot from across the room,
my clothes got soaked and stuck against my skin,
cool-down on a summer afternoon.

Unafraid of darkened skies,
I battled the wind and waded intently uphill,
against the current,
garbage pail covers sailing by
like Frisbees.

Some moments never leave you,
this summer storm on a New Brighton street,
one of them.

I stopped, stood in the midst of a downpour,
and started to spin,
all the while memorizing the sky
in shades of gray.

That day, walking in a storm,

I was freer than I'd ever be again;
since then, every storm's only been bad weather,
and I've been looking out windows
when I should have been out there spinning.

Next storm,
I promise.

Dancing up a Storm

I felt the darkened sky rumbling
like some vast, hungry gut in the distance.
Clouds parted; rain battered the sidewalks,
the kind of rain that bounces.

By the window in silence,
I saw the kids on the porch next door,
safe and dry,
and my mind raced back to a day just like this one
when I sat on a porch, too.

Suddenly, my reverie was broken
by the sound of laughter I believed,
for a moment, was inside my head
until I realized it was outside the window.

There they were,
off the porch, heads tilted toward the sky,
dancing in the downpour,
drenched to the skin.
They held hands and began to spin.

I laughed out loud,
recalling that freedom, glad they'd seized the moment,
wondering if, years from now,
they too would remember the day
they danced up a storm.

"Should we come in?" they shouted up to me.

I thought for a minute and smiled.

"No, keep dancing," I replied. *"There's plenty of time to dry off."*

A lifetime, in fact.

Broken by Love

Summer sky at midnight,
the map of my youthful dreams:
It's like a page of poetry
I memorized and can recite at will,

every star a promise,
spaces between simply unchartered territory,
no wilderness too far to contemplate
as I lay there,
gazing up—
an act of faith.

Back then, tomorrow was the mystery out there,
above me a world
I preferred to this one.

I can smell the grass saturated
with evening,
feel my resolve click into its orbit—
my words were going to blaze across
the sky someday.

Lying there,
I never believed I was,
at that moment,
the best I'd ever be,
but, looking back, maybe I was,

simply because I believed in shooting stars

and never thought about what became of them,
that they were much like a heart
before it is broken
by love.

HEADSTONES

For every page,
a moment lived, lost, and surrendered
to passing time;
and reading the past is a journey
through the darkness and light
that is my life.

To render a reality gone
so vividly you can feel it in every part of you
is a gift,
or so I have been told.

What they fail to say
is that pain is part of the poem,
the moment captured dying
over and over in front of you.

A remembered touch
provides no comfort,
a remembered fire no heat,
and sometimes pages full of words
become headstones,
simple epitaphs that fail to capture
the complexity of human souls.

When I dare journey
through the words that are
all the days of my life,
I realize, far too well,

that revisiting the past
is not reliving it—
it is re-losing it.

Accidental Picasso

My art teacher hated me,
the accidental Picasso I was,
everything I did disproportionate,
lacking depth and perspective.
I couldn't paint, draw, macramé,
or weave a basket.
But I remember the day
I made this leather bracelet .

The smell of tanning fluid
filled my head like helium in a balloon—
turpentine-strong and dizzying
as I stood there, a nondescript piece of leather
in my young hand.

I chose the gold snap
and banged it into place.
A large assortment of stamps
spread before me;
I plucked out
the letters of my name from the set.
One by one, I slammed that hammer
into the top of each metal stamp,
branding the strap and making it mine.
To give it symmetry, I added
two hearts on either side;
then I stained it brown.

Rifling through a drawer, there it was;

I took it out and slipped it on,
this relic of grammar school,
still the symbol to me of the one thing I did right,
recalling how I put this bracelet
before that nun as if to say,
*Look at my name. I know who I am,
and it isn't Picasso.*

The bracelet, you see, still fits;
so does the attitude.

IMPENDING OCTOBER
(For Grandma)

The tug, the lead weight,
of impending October threatens to drag me
into depths I've no desire
to explore again.
You are not there.
From the bridge of elapsing time,
I look behind to what was
and recall the moments I longed to jump
but didn't.
No one could have known what roads
I would traverse to find my way home.
I've walked silently, courageously,
away from the world that was you,
into the life that always awaited me.
When you died,
I was a child without the wisdom to cry,
but as I stared at your cold, waxen face,
I whispered, "Safe journey."
I stand here now and smile,
knowing what you could never come back
to tell me:
There is no such thing
as a safe journey—
only hard-won arrivals.

Color Coordinated

You'd think
I'd be used to this by now,
the voids death leaves behind;
I've been through enough of them.

I walked empty streets at 6:00 a.m.,
an angry child shouting at the sky
for having the audacity to be blue
when gray would have been
more appropriate.

I remember every number
of every hospital room that stole
something from me,
white-washed walls numbing
all but the reality of impending doom.

I recall entering a showroom,
still in shock,
to pick out two caskets
that would lie side by side
in a room that could not contain
all the horror and grief.

I've been in more funeral parlors
than anyone should ever be in,
surrendered more to heaven than I can measure,
said too many goodbyes.
It never gets any easier
to accept the cruelty of the rising sun

and the blue sky
when gray would be more appropriate.

OF ALL THINGS

You always said you'd come back
as a fly—
to zip around or land on walls,
privy to everything.

Why you would pick such an annoying
little reincarnation, I don't know,
but I do know that, every October,
I am surrounded by flies.

This year, you followed me halfway
through the countryside.
Through mountains, by streams and covered bridges
off the beaten path,
I was accompanied by flies,
one landing on my hand, walking softly
over my fingers for much longer than flies
normally do.

I kept wondering,
Is that you?
Could that really be you?

Never sure of whether
to swat or what,
knowing that you always delivered on promises,
I tend to let flies live,
since it's virtually impossible to tell
if those tiny eyes might be blue
like yours.

GULLS

I've had a thing for seagulls
most of my life.
Mesmerized by the motion,
I'd sit silently for hours,
watch blue skies shatter in a flash
of white wings.

Symbols of freedom:
I, too, wanted to soar away
and land on some distant shore,
to cease struggling with questions and dreams
I was never meant to own.

Somehow, I connected to those birds,
beautiful, graceful,
and destined, in spite of that, to be scavengers,
their plight and mine much the same.

At some point, I realized
that, in addition to flight,
gulls have the ability to rise above
and see things, with absolute clarity,
for what they are.

I understood then
why they scream.

Cliff Hanger

On a night like tonight,
we'd be cruising familiar streets,
leaving six-packs under cars,
searching for lighthouses
where there were none,
and laughing.

You hated the songs I loved,
loved the songs I hated,
and ping-pong radio became a sport.
Strange places we found ourselves—
empty parking lots at midnight,
hanging half off a cliff on a summer evening,
a tumbleweed town in Tom's River at 2:00 a.m.

I miss the fuel of reckless abandon,
the common craziness that led us
down uncertain roads.

We may have gone nowhere,
but we arrived together;
dreams may have escaped us,
but we chased them anyway.

I miss gas station stops and bagel breaks,
one-way streets traveled accidentally,
but most of all,
I miss the you and me we used to be
back when we weren't disappointed
when we didn't find the lighthouse,

back when we weren't afraid
of half-hanging off cliffs.

Driven By Joy
(*For Debbie*)

You become this ray of pure light
as you peer through that lens,
totally loosed from this place and time;
the world could vanish, and you'd hardly notice.

In pursuit of an image,
all else fades from view, and nothing matters
but catching the vision exactly as you see it—
in all its color, in all its feeling,
not what it could be but what it is
at that moment.

I love the unconsciousness
of your work, how all of life's worries
fall away,
how your eyes narrow when you see something
and I sit there wondering
what you see that I don't,
and if it will become my next poem
when you laugh and finally point it out
to my untrained eye.

Most people wonder
what I do while you snap away,
why I don't get bored;
I tell them I think best
in the silence of watching you
capture a world so different from the one I see.

One never gets bored in the presence
of a heart driven by joy.
I am firmly convinced that
you are the one who will,
should the sky decide to fall,
capture that blue, magnificent
splintering in one swift click,
and I am determined to be there
in case a star or two happens to fall
with it.

Where the Stars Go

There are warm summer nights
I hang upside down like a bat
from clouds as they float across
my weary eyes.

Caught in a thought, I lose all sense
of the time I'm in,
this moment sacrificed for memories.

Instantly transported to a street corner,
the light on the pole with its halo
blinds me again,
and I hear the sounds of streets
I can still walk with my eyes closed,
the smells of summer,
honeysuckle and little green apples
thudding on grass as they plummeted from limbs
too weak to hold them.

In this room tonight,
far from that fading world,
I wonder if anyone is sitting on my corner,
and I'm tempted to drive there
but don't know what I'm more afraid of:
finding someone,
or discovering only empty space
where once sat a poet
who still hangs upside down from the clouds
and wonders where the stars go
at dawn.

ROOFTOPS

I think often of that kid flying
in the face of everyone who demanded
she get her head out of the clouds,
buffeting herself against every storm that screamed,
No, you can't.
She shut out that sound,
turned the wind into a song.

By windows at midnight,
alone and silent, armed with only a pen,
she peered at the world below,
over rooftops in the distance, aching for words.
She knew they were what she'd spread
across the empty space
like snow on a winter's evening:

a million nights of triumph
when poetry came at the cost of sleep;
other nights of despair when neither happened
and she lived those lonesome hours,
awake and aware.

Having survived the journey
from there to here,
recollecting those rooftops,
new voices from places far beyond them
tell me how my words have touched their hearts,
and I find myself
whispering

Well, kid, you have arrived
for your words have filled the empty space
like snow on a winter's evening.

THE SNOWBALL

Bored to tears and tired of shoveling,
I cursed and muttered about the perils
of growing older.
As I stood on the sidewalk
in a still, silent world,
I was alone,
no one in sight, no one in mind.

Suddenly, I laughed
as an image filled my head, of you,
in your fur-trimmed burgundy coat,
making a snowball.
I waited for you to fling it
and why you placed it carefully on the step was a mystery.
Then, the snowball disappeared
until a sunny day in April
when you removed it from the freezer
and showed it to me—
a moment you'd found a way to preserve
without the words so necessary to me.
I laughed so hard I thought I'd die,
and then, you threw it at me,
something you'd, no doubt, been waiting to do
for months.

It was something only you would've thought of
and only I could've appreciated—
the irony of getting slammed with a snowball in April.

Today, for some reason,
I remembered and laughed until the tears
froze on my face.
Other people keep food in their freezer;
me, I reach in and pull out a memory—
approximate defrost time—
forever.

SAND AND SNOW

Today, for old time's sake,
I sculpted the perfect snowball,
a sleek, circular weapon.

Back then, we built walls,
stockpiled our ammo
and waged war,
dodging, ducking,
plotting an ambush —
always the girls against the boys.
Hours later, flushed and spent,
we'd scoop up white remains
and build a snowman.

In the silence,
like some unspoken ritual,
you and I would roll and place
the pieces one atop the other,
painstakingly smooth them to roundness
as if any of it could prevent
the inevitable.

That was always the problem,
you see:
we built our forevers in the worst of places,
in the sand or out of snow.

Next time we build a snowman,
I say we use cement.

FERRIS WHEEL

Every time I cross the bridge,
a Ferris wheel looms in the distance,
its stillness a grim reminder
of winter's approach.

The sight always returns me
to a humid summer night long ago
when we walked the carnival grounds
and you tried to convince me to take a ride.
I denied you nothing,
but this was different.

You called me a chicken,
and I clucked, glancing at that thing
spinning into the heavens
and wondering what I was afraid of
because, for all intents and purposes,
I wasn't afraid of anything back then.

Last week, as I drove across the bridge
I finally figured it out:
I was afraid, if I reached the sky with you,
the ground would never be good enough again.

DEAD MAN'S HILL

Their screams shatter the winter air
like a pane of glass surrounding the past;
children out for the first real snow,
sleds poised on hilltops.

Dead Man's Hill,
Silver Lake Golf Course,
last hill, far left.
Covered with snow, it loomed,
a huge white monster daring me to try.

I was going down that hill,
one way or another,
and everyone promptly refused
to accompany me on my suicide mission.
I paced for a while
convincing myself I could survive undamaged.

Then I jumped on the sled,
closed my eyes, and listened
as their screams vanished like wispy clouds.
Wind in my face,
speed in my stomach,
I shouted in triumph at the winter sky.

I dragged the sled up the hill,
face flushed with heat and thrill.
I don't know if I was fearless or plain stupid,
but inside the whoosh

of those blades slicing through snow,
a memory formed like an icicle.

Downhill from Here

Lost in time, I re-traced my steps
on the winding paths around the lake.

Blossoms erupting,
a world of pink and white,
I could feel you everywhere
and thought I, too, would burst
from the ache.

Kids rollerblading
down hills I conquered long ago
on my skateboard,
wind in my hair, sun at my back—
the kind of freedom you know once
and never again.

Bittersweet,
the joy of remembering paired
with the knowledge of time's irreversible
forward motion.
I stood by the railing,
watching silver ribbons on the water
that match now the silver in my hair.
I have never felt so old
in my life.

I walked up the hill to our tree
and touched it, something solid
in a world falling apart, a way to remind myself

that goodness, even past,
is still goodness known.

Glancing down, I saw a young boy
pick up speed at the top of the hill
and found myself praying he'd make it—
praying I will, too.

BLACK FENCE

Standing beside it,
waist high or so,
I often contemplated its purpose -
a black iron fence
encircling the lake from end to end.

Not high enough to keep anyone
from climbing over and jumping in,
not attractive enough to be decorative,
it was just there,
a hard surface to lean my body against
as I gazed across the still water
reflecting the sky,
sun dancing across the surface.

If I ran really fast,
I could scrape a stick across the bars
and create a steady rhythm,
like baseball cards in the spokes
of bicycle wheels,
and I did just that when I needed sound
to fill the empty air.

On the platform,
second level,
I'd watch the sunset and fall to silence
as light evaporated, and suddenly
the fence looked blacker than before.

I didn't know then that this is called
a silhouette; I only knew that somehow,
at that time of day,
that black fence took on a magical quality
I never noticed during the afternoon.

Perhaps that is what taught me, in part,
about the magic of shadows
casting themselves in all the bare places
memory learns to fill across the years.

THE DOOR BELL

I hold in my hand
my last physical connection to you;
worn metal, smooth buttons,
names barely legible through
the plastic, scraped and scratched
like the adolescent heart broken
by the sunrise that stole you away.

Tucked away in a pile,
it fell at my feet like a star from the sky,
and I stood, paralyzed by the jolt of recognition.
I could feel memory
blanket me, the music of your voice,
the sound of your walker ticking on the floor
rushed into me and I smiled:

my inheritance, this door bell,
the only shred of your house
left to me through time.
I run my fingers over it
and push the top button,
wondering if it rings somewhere far from here,
if you peek from behind a cloud,
see me, and smile at the sight of me
still trying to gain entry to the invisible door
that will lead me back home to you.

The Dance

Love's slow movement culminates
in a dance of flames,
leaping, meeting, burning
at double intensity.
Painstaking the process
of one heart moving toward another
in the night;
across the room or across the world
it means wading through the debris
to reach into the unknown.
What secrets await in the space
of outstretched arms,
what mysteries are hidden in the folds
of satin dreams—possibilities
that draw you in and move your stubborn feet
closer and closer to your destiny.
And there is destiny in love, you know,
for the dance was choreographed
long before you even heard the music
you've since learned to play with such ease.
There are no accidents in love;
only culminations, meetings and partings,
sound and stillness,
the one, two–three, one, two–three
of love's slow motion
as it finds its rhythm.

Affirmation

To dispel death,
I lie down with life
and, in the motion of your body
find a way to believe
in the pure joy of connection.
To push away the darkness,
I follow the light in your trusting eyes,
knowing it will lead me to a
better place.
In certain moments,
we become electric,
two exposed wires sputtering
and crackling until the right connection
completes the circuit
and lends light to all the corners
I store my heart in.
Your heart beating against my ear
renews my faith in tomorrow,
reminds me that life goes on
in spite of it all;
and so, in the end,
the affirmation of skin gives birth to me,
and I rise from you ready
for whatever another day has in store.

Editing Love

I think
touching you is
like rewriting a poem,
changing words each time to find the
rhythm.

To catch
the rhythm of
a moment is the job
of poets like me and lovers
like you.

Watch as
my fingers force
the margins to expand.
I will take you, I will make you
Epic.

DRESS REHEARSAL

Maybe that's the truth,
that love is not one but many truths
scattered along the way like seeds.
Love is present
in every pair of eyes that have met yours,
in every pair of arms that have held
or have failed to hold you safe
against the tide.
It's in the memory of what was
and what never was,
in every miracle of sunrise you've witnessed,
in every sunset that failed to rid you
of the longing for something more.

Maybe love was never meant to last—
destined to be written in sand, not stone,
and maybe life is simply about learning
how to let go until we get the letting go right.

I've never pretended to understand
what it's all supposed to mean,
but I do believe that love is many truths
spread out along the way like seeds,
and that, if you look behind,
you'll see the garden every tear has nourished,
the bloom of color, the symbol of the courage
it takes to give your heart,
knowing that love is merely
a dress rehearsal for goodbye.

Never Mind the Moon

In a small outdoor cafe,
I heard a father
trying to explain to his daughter
the reason for tides.
The moon, he said,
has a magnetic force the sea responds to.
So the tide rises and falls
according to the moon.

The child seemed satisfied,
but I smiled, thinking about
my own theory.
In my version, it all has to do with ache:
The tide goes out because it cannot bear
the ache of wanting the shore,
and it returns because it cannot bear
goodbye or live without all it has ever known.
In its comings and goings,
it takes the sand as a memory,
a reminder of why it must continue
this exhausting cycle of ebb and flow,
despair and desire.
In spite of itself, it will always come back.

That is what I would have told the child:
The magnetic force is love—
never mind the moon.

THE MUSIC OF MY HEART

This is the music of my heart,
free and easy like the wind,
soft and certain like the sunrise.
Like blood in my veins,
it courses and will not be silenced,
the only suicide that ends
in sound.

This is the melody of my mind,
steady and sad,
full of longing and lifetimes
of unexpressed emotion.
Like the tide of time,
it is the ebb and flow, rise and fall,
of memory unfolding in a tune you will remember
without knowing why.

This is the song of my soul,
words that lead
from the strings of your heart
to the strings of my guitar.
When it catches you off guard
and you wonder what haunting melody
keeps running through your head,
remember this, and only this:
a tune is timeless—
it is love you hum.

Music Lesson

Headphones on,
my own voice blaring in my head,
I contemplate what brings to life, in me,
things I never even know are there.

Easy melodies flow from the strings,
my fingers flying as if I know the tune
long before it is written.

Words fall together in perfect
rhyme and rhythm,
guided by the steady beat of my heart
recollecting you.

I don't know how to read music,
yet it pours from me like a symphony,
the orchestration of unfulfilled desire
I am just now learning how to express.

It amazes me, even now,
the casualness,
the lack of struggle, in giving birth to this music.

When all is said and done,
the answer is simple:

I play you by heart
because I know you by heart.

THE UNRAVELING OF DAYS

Terrible—this wasting
away of a human being,
stooped over so far now
that he almost vanishes into himself.

Death fills the eyes first;
you can read it there
in the blankness,
a place behind them that light
no longer reaches,
the absence of something indefinable,
but an absence all the same.
Your outreached hand
will pass through him like a ghost,
and he cannot see himself
in the mirror,
for shadows are not reflections,
and reflections are reserved
for the living.
I wonder if any semblance of thought passes
through his head,
if he recognizes the unraveling of days
for what it is.
No bridge, perhaps, can span a distance
that is silence.
I only know that, when I look at him,
I become aware of my own breathing,
and it makes me want to climb a tree,
gaze out over the lake

and inhale the sky
as if my life depended on it.

Perhaps it does.

THE THINGS YOU TAUGHT ME

When I was two,
you tightened a Styrofoam belt
around my tiny waist and tossed me in the pool.
I've the photograph to prove it.
This was your way of teaching me to swim.

When I was three,
you laced up my small white skates,
stood me up and pushed me onto the ice
as if I was supposed to know what to do.
At that moment, someone snapped a picture
that turned up in the next day's newspaper.
This was your way of teaching me to skate.

When I was twelve,
you bought two fishing poles,
handed me a worm which I refused to hook,
then told me to drop the line into the water.
When I finally caught something hours later,
you made me throw it back.
This was your way of teaching me to fish.

When I was fifteen,
you pulled a bow and arrow from the closet,
showed me how to load the arrow,
pull back the string,
without warning me to move my arm.
After the archery range,
I was bruised for two weeks.

This was your way of teaching me target practice.

When I was eighteen,
you ordered me into the car,
took me to a parking lot, and made me drive in circles,
telling me to speed up, slow down,
so nervous I couldn't tell the brake from the gas,
screaming at me when I couldn't parallel park
the goddamn car fast enough.
This was your way of teaching me to drive.

When I was thirty-eight,
you went into the hospital and died.
This was your way of teaching me?

EMPTY CLOSETS
(For Dad)

Strange, how poetry manages
to find me in moments
when I need it most;
just when I am about to drown,
a string of words appears
for me to hold on to until I can
catch my breath and get my footing again.
The other night,
frenzied and in need of something to keep me busy,
I decided to clean out your coat closet—
a first step toward acceptance.
One at a time, I took your jackets
off the hangers—
the gray one you last wore to Atlantic City,
the black one I gave you
two Christmases ago,
the smell of your cologne
still lingering on the collars.
I patiently checked every pocket,
hoping to find something,
any small item, that would bring you closer.
I folded each with care,
the recognition of finality growing
as I placed each one neatly in a plastic bag.
I stood there in silence
for the longest time,
lost in thought and empty
like the closet itself now.

Then, I put a piece of tape on the bag,
and as I started to write down the contents,
a small piece of poetry caught me, so
I let it come, smiled, and wrote on the bag:

Dad's Coats.
Pockets Empty—
Of all but the memories.

All The Words in the World

When bridges burn,
the smoke brings tears to your eyes.
Standing on the other side,
you see what's left behind,
but there's no alternate route to lead you back.
We weren't meant to go back.
My booby-trapped life explodes
in places where I least expect it,
and though flames roar, the match
has always been struck by someone else.
Had I ignited it,
I'd have left nothing
recognizable amid the cinders.
I believed once
that words could heal all wounds—
nothing a poem couldn't cure,
no cloud a verse couldn not dispel.
With pen in hand, I was like a god
writing, rewriting endings
to stories whose beginnings
I hadn't even conceived yet.
But life fails to tolerate innocence,
and somewhere along the way,
I learned that even all the words in the world
at my disposal are powerless
to extinguish the flames of bridges
that were meant to burn.
Pens do not extinguish fires;
they only ignite them.

When Seasons Change

In the heart of winter,
in the winter of my heart
is a place untouched by passing years,
forever green and gold like the memories
that abide there.

In the fountains,
cold spray dispersing in the air,
I'm baptized in the laughter
that vanished on the winds of growing.

From a treetop,
I could see what tomorrow would bring,
silver reflections on water blinding me
to harsh realities yet to come.
I dreamed of flying,
unafraid of the distance or the fall;
that is the gift of youth.

On every path, moments bloom;
smiles you gave me,
tears you shed,
words that bled from wounds
you never even knew I hid,
the day I placed a small piece of our mutual time and
space
in a bottle and hurled it
into memory.

Your eyes glistening in the sun
remind me of summer,
the blue skies we will always run beneath,
in my mind, forever young, free, and bound
by dreams as deeply rooted as the trees
that mark all the places we left our hearts
way back before we knew
what time steals
when seasons change.

September Falling

Dwindling light:
Shorter days stretch nights into eternity
and the cold slowly seeps in.

Summer sunsets surrender
to subtler shades of orange,
a tinge of sudden sadness in the air
along with the regrets that passing time cannot erase.

There is a loneliness about autumn,
a heaviness of heart,
the silent burden of loss reflected
in the first leaf that surrenders to the wind.
I never forget that, even as I enjoy
the parade of color dancing
on the breeze—the loss at the center of it all.

When September falls,
it falls and falls and falls
like the heart encountering love;
still it is my favorite season,
an accurate reflection of what it means
to live, to love, to lose in this world.

I appreciate the plight of the leaf
because I understand surrender;
I depend upon the strength of the tree
because I understand survival.
That is perhaps why I can say,

Let winter come paint the world gray;
it is, after all, nothing
that April won't undo.

Spring Thaw

Long walks on short days—
that's what I think of when I look
out at the frozen world;
the silence of twilight descending,
deepening colors of the sky
we strolled beneath,
filling the empty air
with words and laughter,
the cold always outside, never in.
We knew back then as we stood
by the frozen lake
that, with warmer weather, it would
shimmer to life and reflect light again;
we counted on that to get us through
harsh winters when the world
seemed endlessly gray.
I always wanted to skate on that ice,
from one end to the other,
in circles, arms outstretched, face to the wind.

If I fell through, I suppose, I'd have sunk
to the bottom of my childhood and found
my bottle of words also frozen in time,
but I never risked the drowning.
Still, on days like today,
I gaze out my crystallized window,
think of long walks on short days,
and feel the desire to skate away
in ways I never did then,

thankful that, in spite of it all,
some part of me still believes
in spring thaw.

TODAY'S LESSON
(For Kimberly)

Lost in youthful freedom,
they know of the world
only the space between
the headphones.

They reek of invincibility,
oblivion cached in their back packs,
somewhere between books they never open
and pens dried up
from disuse.

On days when the chatter is ceaseless,
I am tempted to tell them your story—
how you politely requested a place
in the class and worked diligently
in the second chair from the door,
how you vanished silently one month later
and became a headline.

Burned, you were, by your own invincibility
and a trusting heart,
lost in your youthful freedom
just like them.
What you might have been died with you,
your potential turned to ashes
by an animal with no potential of his own.

I remember those headlines,

I remember the silence
after I made the announcement
of your murder,
how we all walked out of the room
a little sadder, a little wiser.

I look at the faces before me now
and wonder how I can teach them
to respect life and appreciate knowledge,
to make them understand
the lesson of the empty chair
where you should be sitting.

A Million Dreams
(For Justina)

Behold this gaping wound
in the earth,
a bloodless gash in green grass,
the symbol of so many broken hearts,
this empty hole that will hold you now for all eternity
the way no lover's arms ever could have.
You will be safe here,
protected from life's misery;
there is so much you will never know
and I'm not sure if that's good or bad.
Beautiful and nineteen,
a whole life to plan,
a million dreams of tomorrow
wiped out in an instant
through no fault of your own,
those dreams must have raced
before you in those final seconds
before the world exploded into a bright light
and you died on the street
in the cold black night,
the victim of a stranger who had no respect for his life or yours.

I mourn another empty chair in the classroom,
remember our last conversation
the morning of the day you died,
about a research paper you never got to write.
But I will always remember, Justina—
I will always remember

and pray that the million dreams you took with you
will blossom into spring daisies
and brighten the world again.

More Tree than Flower

Once, I believed I'd simply blow away
if the wind was strong enough.
Fragmented, I prayed I could
hold the pieces together long enough
to survive winter storms.
There were times when I had to touch
a hard surface,
a door, a window,
to make sure I was real,
not just another phantom
of my own imagination.
I watched flowers bend
beneath a downpour
and saw, in them,
my human condition—
needing the nourishment
but afraid of the torrent.
Was that me, I wondered,
fragile and prey to any storm on the horizon?
In that instant, I knew
safety was just an illusion;
I built walls only to find
vulnerability inside.
I've learned a lot since then,
when the wind was my worst enemy.
I am more tree than flower, it seems,
and trees may bend, may break—
but they seldom blow away.

SYNCHRONIZED SWIMMING

For a moment,
all motion ceases
as they rest in still water,
staring in perfect contentment
like lovers catching sight of each other
across a room.

I watch, an uninvited stranger,
this odd, repetitive ritual
of what I assume to be love.

Slowly, the water ripples
from the bottom up
as they begin their dance—
one swimming softly left,
the other circling right
until they meet in the middle again.

They achieve perfect harmony,
synchronized swimmers
who know each other's motions
before they happen
and trust memory alone will lead them
to that moment of still water.

They are like us—
the wall of glass between them,
no interruption of love;
they flutter in separate water

and dream of the ocean
where they can escape boundaries
and swim away together
by the light of a setting sun.

TO SAY THE LEAST

My first taste of love was longing—
admire but don't desire,
look but don't touch.
You were beauty in motion,
irresistible, unattainable,
except in words that poured from me
and netted you in ways nothing else could.

My first awareness
of the ache that was you
filled all my empty spaces
like stars in a velvet sky.

My last taste of love, too, was longing—
where desire and admiration
merged in the kiss of a lifetime,
when look surrendered to touch,
tender as the night falling.
For a moment,
you were beauty suspended,
the butterfly that landed briefly, softly,
on my cheek,
then left like a whisper.

I burned for you
from the start before the start,
and I burn for you still,
steady as a candle in a lonely room;
but it's hard, to say the least,

to return to darkness,
and love the cold again,
once you've held the fire of another heart
in your hands.

HEART BEAT IN THE HOLLOW

I play in the dark
like there is no tomorrow,
chord after chord,
these tunes that sprang from
a part of me I've lost
along the way to here.

Amid the strumming,
new fragments surface,
but I cannot find the right order,
a way to string the notes together
to make of the emptiness
a song worth remembering at dawn.

I hold my guitar close enough
to feel my heart beat in the hollow
so I'm reminded that I have survived
more lonelinesses than I can count;
always words have blossomed
in the desert of my soul,
and this moment is no different.

I know these six strings intimately,
felt them vibrate beneath my touch,
made permanent their fleeting sounds.
I play in the dark
like there is no tomorrow
because there isn't;
there's only yesterday and you,

and the sweet, plaintive sound
of this guitar crying
in the night.

Can you hear it?

HOLDING THE LIGHT

Some moments become monuments
erected permanently in the mind.
I know them instinctively as they unfold,
the poet's eye keen to unwritten words.

I see you and little you
illuminated by a rising moon,
your motion on the grass,
fluid like wind through trees.
You are chasing fireflies,
trying to capture one,
and I watch,
totally entranced by the sight.

Both of you run to and fro,
this way and that,
frustrated by what keeps escaping you.
A tiny light appears for a moment,
then disappears,
and by the time you near it,
it reappears somewhere else.

I get up and, with a flashlight,
see the magic bug and grab it.
She's so excited as I place it in her hand;
after all, she's holding light.
Unhappy when the light flies away,
she immediately asks me to get another one.

I smile at her, look at you,
and hope she never loses her ability
to hold the light
even though she knows that it will fly away.
I pray she always trusts, as you do,
despite logical explanations,
in the magic of fireflies and moon rise.

TUMBLING THROUGH CENTURIES

In my hand,
I hold what could be
a champagne-bottle shard from some grand hotel
that went up in flames
and was swept into the sea.

This might be
the topper to a bottle of poison
used to murder a king
or settle a lover's quarrel,
or medicine from an apothecary,
an antidote that saved a million lives
or only one.

This could be
the piece of a glass
two lovers sipped wine from
on a romantic evening,
candles burning all around them,
as they swore to each other
till morning.

There are lives here
in this rainbow of fragments,
frosted by tumbling through centuries,
a secret history
narrated by the whispers of the water,
if you listen closely.

I pick up these pieces of glass
and turn them, like the tide,
over and over in my hands,
as if somehow they will reveal
their stories,
all the memories
that don't belong to me
sequestered in a bottle
that is its own message.

NEVER FAR
(For Uncle Tony and Aunt Ann)

Sirens on the summer wind,
crying of the night that stole the stars
and left a black hole in me:
They are memories bathed in the blood
of innocents and innocence,
crimson tide that still visits my dreams,

voices, intonations,
words clear even now
that simply could not express or grasp
the shattering of the world as I knew it.
I recall the wave of nausea,
my body shaking as if electrified,
the scream in my own head
echoing inside a cave of denial.

Air saturated with heat,
I could barely breathe,
half-wished I wouldn't
because to inhale meant to take in
the reality in all its horror and sorrow.

Many nights have changed me,
but not like that one twenty years ago
when the heart of me went out
of the heart of me.
Evil triumphed that night
when two gentle souls perished

in a storm of rage.

Despite the passing time,
I'm never far from there,
never far from those sirens
on the summer wind,
so unlike any song I've ever heard
or written.

TESTAMENT

Behold these pages pushed out of me
like some repetitive, awesome delivery,
the final fruits of my labor
in black and white.

No one can know
how tears fell with words sometimes,
and I didn't know
if I was crying for the loss of their lives
or my own as I knew it.

Night after night,
and well into the night,
I pounded out the story,
keeping the darkness at bay,
making meaning out of nothingness.

These pages are a testament
to my own survival,
the survival of memory,
the triumph of love over loss.

They're an eternal gift to those
who never failed to believe in me,
or to remind me
that morning was always and only
a whisper away
no matter how dark the dark.

The Dark Shape of Trees

Countless car windows
I've silently stared through
at the dark shape of trees
against the sky at twilight.

There is that moment,
world poised
on the edge of night,
when the sky's still light enough to serve
as backdrop to shadowy limbs
reaching into seemingly empty space.

First time I noticed them,
I was on a highway in Pennsylvania,
heading home,
and my eyes fixed themselves so tightly
on trees whizzing by,
I saw the images hours later
as I closed my eyes in sleep.
I didn't understand why I was so drawn,
so captured, but the habit
stayed with me.

I've traveled many roads since then,
highways, byways, streets
that don't exist on maps,
only now, I understand what escaped me then:

nothing ominous or profound here,

just something resolute
about the dark shape of trees
against the sky at twilight,
a message about permanence
in a world I feel I am seeing, most times,
through the window of a vehicle
speeding ever closer
to the edge.

A Gift to the Stars

On ink-stained summer nights,
you'd find me,
set off from the others
(like a parenthesis)
writing in a notebook or
on some scrap of paper
secreted in my back pocket
just for the occasion of a poem—

with the sinking sun,
the rise of words to the surface,
sea shards thrown up from the depths
of who I was and couldn't be.
I scribbled in blues, pinks, and lavenders
until it felt like the evening sky
was simply running down the pages.

Mood wasn't something I waited for,
it was the way I lived,
open to the world as poetry in the offing.

I need to get back to that time
when I built bridges instead of walls
and faith was as simple as a song
on the wind.

Tonight, it's just me
(still a parenthesis)
and these pages,

face to face once again;
perhaps, I'll do what I did so many times then—
write a poem on a scrap of paper,
tear it to pieces, throw it up in the air
as a gift to the stars,
and watch it rain poetry
on this ink-stained summer night.

No Ghost

Thirty-five years down the line,
his, like the face on a coin,
remains embossed on my mind.
His hair, the color of straw,
his skin so alabaster he was nearly invisible in sunlight,
we called him "Casper,"
one of the nicer names he acquired.

Effeminate, limp-wristed, and swishy,
he lived to annoy, sashaying down the sidewalk
like some model on a runway.
Voices rose, became a chant,
spilled out the school bus windows—
Fag-got, Fag-got, Fag-got,
my own voice part of the thoughtless, robotic chorus.

The day he put his finger in my face,
some floodgate in me broke,
and I beat the hell out of him.
Such rage for a twelve-year-old
makes me wonder now
if I was beating him or me.

In the sunlight,
I saw veins through his skin
and stopped my fist in mid-air,
glanced at the crowd cheering me on,
rose, and extended my hand to help him up.

I went off alone,
changed in that moment,
by blue veins pumping blood
beneath alabaster skin—
the me I saw in his defiant, pale-blue eyes.

Next morning,
as he stepped on the bus,
everyone calling him Casper,
I looked at him and said the words
I should have said all along:

"Hello, Steven."

The Promise of Bridges

I don't know the moment
when the car lurches to a stop
in the middle of the bridge
and someone rushes out,
motor running, door open,
and flings himself, like a human Frisbee,
into the air.

Reading newspaper reports,
I've wondered if that decision's already made
or if the span just presents
an instant opportunity
for the tortured soul inside the car
trying to find reasons
to keep breathing.

I've walked that edge,
felt the pull toward oblivion,
sat in the passenger's seat
glancing out the window over the rail
at the long drop to the slate blue
water beneath,
and wondered, What exactly
is the promise of bridges?

Whether we cross them or leap,
we still get where we intend to go.

But is there a moment

after the leap when, falling fast and hard,
one turns to face
the astounding blue of the sky
just one more time
before

LATITUDE

In Barrow,
northernmost part of Alaska,
the sun doesn't rise for 67 days.

To occupy that much night is an art,
to fill that kind of darkness
the mission of poets.

What happens when night falls and falls,
when daylight fails and fails
to arrive, altering the sense of time
our lives rely on?

More time to dream
on the edge of perpetual evening;
more time to study the stars
and discover the truth about wishing;
more time to stare into a candle's flame
and recognize how close to darkness
we always are anyway.

But what is night
without the promise of dawn?

I can tell you it's no place for words to wander,
a place a million candles cannot warm or transform.

I've never been to Alaska,
but I've learned about night without end

just the same—
every night without you.

Magnificent Desolation

were the words Buzz Aldrin used
to describe the landscape of the moon.

I was 8 when Armstrong uttered
his famous words,
and all I remember of the coverage
was how silly it seemed
to put a flag in a place where no one
would say the Pledge of Allegiance.
What did it all have to do with me anyway,
this venture into space?

Forty years later,
I understand.
Watching the actual film last week,
hearing the scratchy words
traveling 240,000 miles through still air,
I smiled at how beautiful Earth looked
from that distance—
peaceful and blue,
void of all ugliness.

I know all about magnificent desolation,
the landscape of the moon and the heart
not so different,
and as for giant leaps,
I've taken a few of those myself -
moments when what could be and what is
aligned in one blinding moment

of realization.

I know precisely what I'd have said
if I'd landed on the moon:
I'm staying.

Graffiti on the Sky

We all write against the dark;
graffiti on the face of the sky,
when interposed by a star,
becomes a poem,
nothing more, nothing less
than a cry.

We all scribble
against the schizophrenic voices
of a world gone mad,
sound rushing past and through us
like a scream on the wind
whose meaning we can barely capture.

We're all pirates pillaging the pockets of day
for a gold coin to imprint ourselves upon,
then for a way to spend ourselves
that leaves something behind,
a measure of our worth
for someone else to contemplate.

If you're a poet,
you always write against the dark and wait,
just wait,
for a star to interpose.

What a Poem Feels Like

sensation in the soul,
the needles and pins of
a numb limb awakening,
simultaneous push toward movement
to overcome discomfort and immobility
to avoid it—
that is the feeling of a poem.

every moment's premonition,
pieces of future,
disconnected, unrealized,
the unworded that will be reworded
when time ripens the memory
and it falls upon the poet's head
like an apple in autumn.

space, not empty but vast
like a canvas of sky stretched taut
across the night,
full, not of holes, but accommodations
for stars;
deceptive distance, the horizon,
the line of sea and sky
much further away than it seems,
wisps of dreams lost;
this is what a poem feels like—
trying to capture a cloud
on the tip of pen.

The First Sound
(In memory of Nicky, September 11, 2001)

Spare yourself the wondering
about last moments—
if he knew what was happening,
if he felt the earth shake beneath him,
if he suffered or slid painlessly away.

I know the despair of uncertainty,
the haunting images that keep you
awake and pacing floors late into the night,
the scream you dare not express,
afraid that, if you start,
you'll never stop.

Forever linked to unspeakable horror,
it's hard now to separate his life,
your memories from your imaginings
of what his dying was like.
In time, you'll see his life was far more,
that the way he died must never
overshadow the courage with which he lived,
or you will lose him again and again.

Believe his last thoughts were of you,
the memories you made through his growing,
and somewhere, in the midst of it all,
he became the man he was meant to be,
if even for a brief moment;
know that upon leaving this world,

his deafness lifted like a veil
and the first sound Nicky ever heard
was not the breaking of glass
or the roar of concrete collapsing,
but the music of the heavens,
the voice of God singing him home.

Stranger to Stranger
(In memory of Annie Le)

I don't have to see your eyes to know
that suffering resides where joy abided
only weeks ago.

I've traversed the geography of your nights,
the terrain of uncertainty and horror
you maneuver,
breathless in wondering about those final moments
and the fluttering of the heart you loved
before it stopped beating and the light left her eyes.

You'll relive your last conversation
till it becomes a film unraveling in your head,
as if memorizing the ordinary dialogue
will keep her here and safe from harm.

You sit there,
devastated and forlorn,
on this day when you should be
carrying her over the threshold
into a new life, and instead,
watch them carry her casket to a home you can't live in;
you wear the wedding band
she never got to place upon your finger
as an act of faith, married to this sorrow now,
all the days of your life.

Stranger to stranger,

I know your eyes for having seen them
staring back at me from the mirror
of my own sorrow so long ago.

Carry her gently through time
and she will stay with you as she was,
your memories immune to the violence
of her leaving.

There really are some things
intolerable cruelty cannot kill—
and love, yes love,
is one of them.

Where Mountains Weep

Rocky sweeps on either side,
we ride the highway in between.
My eyes catch sight
of water trickling down
on top of icicles that cling
to the sides of mountains—

an amazing sight
most people wouldn't notice,
except that somehow it's me I see—
the part of me frozen still,
ice cold, granite hard,
crystallized by life;
and the other part
melting so easily,
I couldn't fight it
even if I wanted to.
Suddenly loosed by you,
I run like that water
off the edges of cliffs,
aware of the ice beneath
that is also me, and pray for
the wisdom of summer.

It's like that here,
where roads cut through rock
the way a kiss
cut through my heart of stone.

Stay with me here,
in this place where mountains weep,
where I don't.

Undiluted Starlight

There's a place on the edge
of a silent, solitary field, tonight,
snow resplendent in moonlight,
where wind crosses the line into song.

Here lives a lonesomeness
totally void of loneliness,
starlight undiluted by streetlights or headlights,
only darkness falling softly.

In a world full of anguish,
there's a space of peace,
the greatness of the universe palpable
as I sit cross-legged on the cold ground
and feel the heartbeat of the earth
beneath me,
through me.

In time, the body goes numb
in the biting cold,
but my mind is totally alive,
sight and insight clearer than ever,
as I live fully in the moment,
loosed from the past,
indifferent to the future.

There's a place on the edge
of a silent, solitary field,

snow resplendent in moonlight,
where I sit, tonight, and listen
as wind crosses the line into song
and I write the words,
praying they'll reach you wherever you are
and lead you to me
so I can hand you this gift of undiluted starlight,
as if it is mine to give.

The Symphony of Trees

I return to the pages
with renewed desire
to capture and captivate;
like coming home after long absence,
the eye sees with striking suddenness
what's gone unnoticed.

We inhale but seldom take in
anything other than air;
our exhalation does not alter seasons
like the wind.

I've learned in this absence
from words to watch the wind—
how it begins in a small swirl,
the slightest hint observed
in leaves whispering across the ground;
how it absorbs the power of the sky,
the circle widens and lifts the ground
off itself;
how it whips itself into a frenzy
until it is high enough
to conduct a symphony of trees,
the orchestration of nature no human hand
can replicate.

The real gift of living
is not simply living;
it's living simply enough
to recognize in your own breathing

your connection to the poetry
that is the wind.

About Tulips

Tight in the bud,
it's hard to believe
this green thing will suddenly burst
into flower in a day or two—
well protected,
totally closed in upon itself,
impervious to elements
that will damage its chances
of ever seeing the sun.

Then, in an act of absolute faith
it becomes a magnificent flower,
all it was meant to be,
every mood painted on its petals—
the fiery red, passionate purple,
mellow yellow colors of Spring
there for the world to see.

There is much humanity
in the growth of a tulip,
in its movement from bud to blossom;
but there's also its fatal flaw,
for tulips just don't open—
they open themselves completely,
totally exposed inside and out
to the weather, to the world
that is far from kind to fragile things.

And that's why they die so fast;
that's why.

ECLIPSE OF REASON

Ruled by logic
almost all my life,
my head controlled my heart
except in dreams
where roaming was safe.

Feeling was forbidden,
the opponent I could beat back only with words
on pages;
it was the whispering I drowned with ink,
reasoning myself out of commitment and complication,
as adept at denial as I was at the poetry
that captured it.

My first lapse in reason
was disaster. I spent more time
convincing myself I believed in forever
than I did feeling it;
I grew weary of picking up the pieces of myself,
slamming the door behind me,
reaffirming myself to myself.

My second lapse was more, far more—
a total eclipse of reason,
throwing myself firmly against
the winds of impossibility,
rising like the tide above fear to discover
that we carry within us one love
that defies logic.

The sun rose in an instant
with the touch that made everything in me dance,
and I learned that when you let your heart
rule your head,
you can actually fall head over heels
without hurting yourself.

PIECES OF YOU
(For M.C.)

Stray photographs,
scattered notes falling
from books—
cleaning out I keep finding
pieces of you
as accidental as the collision
of my life with yours.

In my hands today,
a notebook,
Italian lessons from the semester
we met,
the familiar cursive cutting into me
as it did into the yellowing pages.

I discarded that whole notebook,
ripping page after page
away from the spiral,
tearing it to shreds,
angry that I was angry
even now after all this time.

I've no definition of you.
I found myself with you,
lost myself to you,
nearly killed myself
to escape you.
You challenged me to take hold
of my life, of who I was
and wanted to be,

and I did that the day I left.
Now, I pick up these pieces of you,
and still don't know what to call you
except
gone.

GEOGRAPHY OF MY EXISTENCE

My first foray onto the streets of Brooklyn
since my days with you,
memories around corners,
ghosts of both the dead and living
abound.

You forced me to drive
over that bridge and into that world,
to learn the music of those noisy streets
and distinguish the moods
of horns honking.

I learned the streets of Bay Ridge
by circling endlessly in search of a place
to park,
walking to the corner store
or celebrating the Third Avenue festival.

You broadened
the geography of my existence
by forcing me out
of the boundaries I lived inside.
It called for a braver heart,
a more fearless approach
to travel in your world,
and I became braver, stronger, surer
of what I could and couldn't do.

The other day

it was me who found the way home from Brooklyn,
driving with certainty of direction
in the pouring rain,
following my instincts
and my memory to the bridge
you made part of my journey so long ago—

the only bridge, in fact, we didn't burn.

ETERNITY

Winter night descends,
a rich, black velvet curtain
out of whose deep folds
fall a million twinkling stars
that electrify the air.

Bespeckled and still,
the shimmering moment fades
into memory
as the words to capture it
form and hang like icicles.

That's what poets do—
take icicles in the mind,
fire them with a pen
until they melt, re-form
on pages, into stone.

The rescued moment
knows not the oblivion
of swift passing time
and makes, of this shimmering
Vermont night, an eternity.

INTERLUDE OF RAIN

Interlude of rain
tap-dancing on the still leaves,
the pitter-patter
of autumn sky's tiny feet
perfecting a midnight waltz.

I stand, a shadow
against a small wood cabin
between woods and creek
listening to the rhythm
no man-made song can copy—

The rapid pace to soft and slow
till all sound ceases
and the mist rises from the grass
like the memory of a kiss.

WHERE QUARRELS END

What greatness lay here
beneath the hard frozen ground—
the wordless, mute bones
of the unforgotten dead
poet versed in country things.

Windswept autumn leaves
dance across the dark granite
bearing names and dates,
a legacy carved in stone
more permanent than a poem.

Arrows point the way
through narrow and silent paths
margined by gravestones
with names obliterated
as if erased from paper.

You find a stone
instead of a monument,
hardly a tribute
to one of America's
still echoing great voices.

Then again, it seems
that Robert Lee Frost realized
all lover's quarrels
end somewhere between a poem
and quiet country grave yards.

Choreography

Behold this canvas in motion,
canopy of deep blue and white
like a dome protecting
the countryside beneath.

Fast-moving sky
above a slow-moving world
where water falls and trips
over rocks on the edges
of backwoods roads.

The clouds cast shadows on mountains
like a smile disappearing
from a face suddenly overtaken
by contemplation.

In the momentary dance
of day sinking to gold
against gray limbs of air on air,
branches of fog,
one can find a heaven to believe in
in the awesome choreography
that is the Vermont sky.

Pennies from Heaven

Water ends;
land begins and heaves itself
into a sky seeping orange
like paint running down a canvas
onto the surface of a lake,
day poised on the edge of evening.

Still and silent,
this is the moment of transition,
the empty elegance of blue
finding its way to lavender-orange
of necessary endings.

Leaves, silhouetted against fading light,
ruffle, flutter, in the breeze
like feathers of ducks shaking off water.

No brush can replicate this,
no words can adequately capture this perfection—
that's best left
to the eye behind the shutter,
the mind behind the memory;
glittering, copper light
ripples beneath the water
like a million newly-minted
pennies from heaven
you simply don't have enough pockets for
and so can only carry away and suspend in thought,
temporarily,
like a leaf loosed in the wind.

Paper

To pick up a pen
and softly crack open a moment
is sacred,
an act imbued with faith that something's
worth finding there.

A silence,
the kind I felt, once, as I sat
in a empty church alone with my godlessness,
accompanies the first stroke,
as I anoint the page with ink.

I've written hymns to the sky,
requiems for the living dead,
performed some miracles of my own,
worshiped on altars of stone
and wrote words there, too.

No prohibitions in my church,
no forsaken acts to renounce
or sinners to be saved here,
just one soul,
emerging from the dark,
standing in the light of a white page.

When I bend my head,
it is not to pray,
it is to write—
paper the only god who ever listened,

words the only religion
I've ever had faith in,
what I found in the sand
instead of that second set of footprints.
I pick up this pen,
feel the sanctity of what I am about to do,
and know what it means
to believe.

Tangible Remains

Because I stole them from the sea,
they're part of me,
salvaged from a past that is no more.
Memory solidified, they're pieces of dreams
I had before the wave of being
turned me upside down and pulled me under.

I read our common fate
rounded, smoothed, blunted
by unpredictable tides.
I don't know their points of origin
or where they might have gone
had I not picked them up—
their history is written on them just the same.

Some would say they're simply
shards of glass smoothed by the sea,
but they're far more;
they are the tangible remains
of a million cracked illusions
discovered along the shores of growing.

And of the past,
they're what I choose to keep,
choose to recall—
these shards, so blue and green and white,
of my survival.

About the Author

Linda Principe is an adjunct professor of English at the College of Staten Island, where she has taught writing and literature for the last twenty-four years. She is also a freelance writer and editor. She is the author of *Surviving Murder: A True-Crime Memoir,* which recounts the harrowing murders of her aunt and uncle by their son. Writing poetry since the age of thirteen, her poems have appeared, through the years, in a variety of publications. *Tangible Remains* is her first poetry collection. In her spare time, she enjoys reading, playing the guitar, songwriting, and collecting seaglass.

www.ingramcontent.com/pod-product-compliance
Lightning Source LLC
Chambersburg PA
CBHW051802040426
42446CB00007B/484